ASTON MARTIN

Richard Loveys

ASTON MARTIN HERITAGE TRUST

Published in Great Britain in 2015 by Shire Publications Ltd, PO Box 883, Oxford, OX1 9PL, UK.

PO Box 3985, New York, NY 10185-3985, USA.

E-mail: shire@shirebooks.co.uk
www.shirebooks.co.uk

A CIP catalogue record for this book is available from the British Library.

Shire Library no. 819.   ISBN-13: 978 0 74781 505 1

PDF e-book ISBN: 9781784420741

ePub ISBN: 9781784420734

Richard Loveys has asserted his right under the Copyright, Designs and Patents Act, 1988, to be identified as the author of this book.

Typeset in Garamond Pro and Gill Sans.

Printed in China through Worldprint Ltd.

15 16 17 18 19   10 9 8 7 6 5 4 3 2 1

COVER IMAGE
Cover design by Peter Ashley, photography of a detail of an Aston Martin DB5 by Glynn Downing. Back cover: Aston Martin badge, 1930–2.

TITLE PAGE IMAGE
Aston Martin DB5 convertible, 1963. A publicity picture used by the company.

CONTENTS PAGE IMAGE
The oldest surviving Aston Martin (the 1921 A3) and one of the newest (the 2013 Vanquish) outside Aston Martin's factory at Gaydon, Warwickshire. The special logo which marked the centenary year is on the right.

ACKNOWLEDGEMENTS
I would like to thank all the people from the Aston Martin Heritage Trust (AMHT) and the Aston Martin Owners Club (AMOC) who gave help, advice and encouragement for the preparation of this publication. Valuable help with the text was given by the Trust's Registrar, Tim Cottingham, and by Roger Carey, Terry Farebrother, David Lewington, Neil Murray, Jon Radgick, Kingsley Riding-Felce and Rob Smith.

The images (unless stated otherwise) were provided by the Trust's archivist, Donna Bannister, who – as always – was extremely helpful. The Trust's archive includes a large collection of images, many of which originated from Aston Martin Lagonda and its predecessor companies. The Trust now owns the copyright of these images. Other images were provided by: Alamy, pages 38, 46, 55, 58 and 59; Rex Gray, page 24 (top); Philip Hooper, page 7 (bottom); David Lewington, page 29; Rob Smith, page 41 (top); Wikicommons/Kurush Pawar, page 43; Wikcommons/Fabrice Pluchet, page 45 (top); Wikicommons/Alexandre Prévot, pages 45 (bottom) and 48 (bottom).

Any errors which remain are entirely the author's responsibility.

This book is published by Shire Publications on behalf of the Aston Martin Heritage Trust. The author is a Trustee of the AMHT and a long-standing member of the AMOC. He has been an owner of an Aston Martin for many years and is also a keen builder of model Aston Martins.

CONTENTS

IN THE BEGINNING: 1913–47

IN 1912 LIONEL MARTIN and Robert Bamford formed a business partnership and began selling Singer cars from premises in Henniker Place, South Kensington. Their aim was to produce a car 'for the discerning owner driver, with fast touring in mind'.

On 15 January 1913 Bamford and Martin Ltd (B&M) was established as 'dealers in, manufacturers and repairers of Motor cars'; this was the company that grew into Aston Martin Lagonda Ltd. The company's history includes technical innovation, outstanding cars, international racing success as well as financial difficulties, and, according to Simon de Burton, writing in *The Aston Martin Yearbook* of 2013, it has survived owing to four reasons: 'a knack for making fabulous cars, a deal of luck, lots of respect and, above all, that thoroughbred Britishness that simply doesn't recognise defeat'.

Lionel Martin believed that competition improved the products and helped sales; accordingly much effort was devoted to events such as trials and hill climbs. He himself drove in most of these. The cars which left the Singer factory able to achieve some 40 mph were lapping Brooklands at 70 mph after Bamford and Martin's improvements. Particular success was achieved with the Singers at the Aston Hill climb, in Buckinghamshire. It is now a public road, and B&M's involvement is marked by a cairn erected in 1997. Many customers asked for their Singers to be similarly modified and as a result B&M decided to manufacture their own cars.

Cars like these, exhibited at the 1935 Olympia Motor Show, were among the last ones that Aston Martin produced with its 1½ litre engine.

Right:
Lionel Martin,
one of the
founders of the
company.

Far Right:
Bamford
and Martin's
certificate of
incorporation,
15 January 1913.

A prototype to the company's specification was tested in 1914 using an Isotta Fraschini chassis and a Coventry Simplex engine. In 1914 the cars were named Aston-Martins (with the hyphen) to commemorate the competition successes, and to put them high in alphabetical lists.

The first Aston-Martin was registered in 1915; known as Coal Scuttle, it was the second car built by the company and used a revised Coventry Simplex engine. The car was employed extensively for development and competition.

Coal Scuttle on
the Nailsworth
Ladder hill climb
in the Cotswolds,
driven by Lionel
Martin.

By this time the company was engaged in work related to the First World War.

In 1919 B&M was again active in competitions using Coal Scuttle as well as continuing to sell Singers. Producing its own cars required larger premises and in early 1920 the company moved to Abingdon Road, off Kensington High Street. The second Aston-Martin was registered at the end of 1920. At about this time Robert Bamford resigned from the company; his place was taken by Mrs Kate Martin.

Five cars were built in 1920 and 1921, using a variety of engines and bodies, and were for development rather than for sale to customers, with only rear wheel brakes, and Sankey wheels. One of these, chassis A3, is the oldest surviving Aston Martin and now belongs to the Aston Martin Heritage Trust. In 1923 A3 became the first B&M car sold to a private owner. Another of this batch was known as Bunny and had a successful competition career including hill climbs, Brooklands races, world records and sixth place in the GP des Voiturettes at Le Mans in 1921. These five cars originally used their own 1½-litre side-valve engines. B&M followed the accepted

The car badge used by Bamford and Martin.

A3, built in 1921, is the oldest surviving Aston-Martin and is now owned by the Aston Martin Heritage Trust.

practice of the time in swapping engines, registration numbers and bodies between cars when required. B&M continued development, testing and competition but sold few cars as it was concentrating on perfecting its designs.

In the early 1920s Count Louis Zborowski, a well-known racer, was competing in an Aston-Martin. In 1922 he invested in the company to enable it to continue in competitions and to assist production of customer vehicles. Two cars were built for the Strasbourg Grand Prix in 1922 with twin camshaft 16-valve 1½-litre engines; both retired but performed well in the 2-litre class. One, later known as Green Pea, was driven by Zborowski; it still races today. The two GP cars were some of the first to use the well-proportioned radiators which are a feature of so many Aston-Martins.

Financial difficulties caused the sale of several of the company's development and racing cars late in 1922. In that year the first new cars sold to the public were produced. They were made with either the Standard or the Sports chassis and most had the side-valve engine. The bodies were constructed by various coachbuilders as B&M did not have sufficient resources; this was the custom at the time. The following year a special single-seater was built, which aimed to be the first light

The 1922 Strasbourg Grand Prix cars; Clive Gallop is behind the steering wheel in number 8 and Count Louis Zborowski is the driver for number 15.

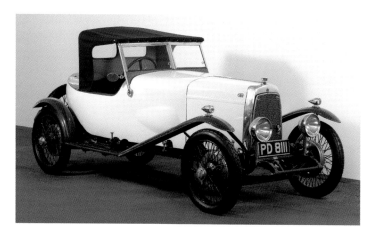

An early three-seater car with the side-valve engine. It was built using the chassis and other parts from a racing car which crashed while being towed from the coachbuilder.

car to cover 100 miles in one hour; the vehicle was called Razor Blade because it was so narrow. Tyre failure prevented the car from achieving its target. Razor Blade now usually lives at the Brooklands Museum, and can sometimes be seen in action.

Production and the sale of cars continued, most of them powered by the company's side-valve engine. Many private owners used their Aston-Martins in competitions, which helped to enhance the company's reputation. Cars were built using two chassis lengths and with open or closed bodywork. Virtually no two B&M cars delivered to customers were the same: the chassis might have common characteristics but the coachwork was made to the customers' specification.

In 1923 B&M was in severe financial difficulties, which were compounded when Louis Zborowski was killed the following year driving a Mercedes in the Italian Grand Prix. Lady Charnwood, whose son (the Hon. John Benson) had started work with the company, stepped in to provide essential capital, and some financial restructuring ensued. B&M was then bought by Lady Charnwood and her son became a director. The company exhibited at the 1925 Olympia Motor Show, but was again overcome by financial difficulties as a result of poor sales. A receiver was appointed, and B&M closed. Just over sixty cars had been built by 1925.

A. C. Bertelli, who led the company in the 1930s, was a talented engineer and racing driver.

In 1924 William Renwick and A. C. (Bert) Bertelli founded Renwick and Bertelli Ltd, based in Birmingham. The company intended to design and build a four-cylinder 1½-litre overhead camshaft engine for sale to car manufacturers. One of the first people to be employed was the talented engineer and draughtsman Claude Hill; he stayed for some twenty-five years. A prototype vehicle was built to test the engine, registered in 1926.

The availability of Aston-Martin offered Renwick and Bertelli a unique opportunity to expand into car manufacturing, and capitalise on the superb reputation for high quality and competition success for which Lionel Martin and others had invested so much money. Renwick and Bertelli bought the business late in 1926, named it Aston Martin Motors Ltd, and moved it to Victoria Road in Feltham, west of London. Next door a coachbuilding business was established by Bert's brother Harry which designed and built most of the bodies for the cars that were made over the next few years.

The company began the process of designing the parts needed to build a new car. It was soon found – as it had been by Lionel Martin – that many of these had to be manufactured by contractors as the company did not have capacity to make everything. Probably the only item carried over from the B&M cars was the radiator with the original badge: several had come with B&M's assets.

The earliest Aston Martins from this new company are known as the First Series; the gearboxes were separate from the engines and the rear axles had worm drive gears. The initial cars were ready for the 1927 Olympia Motor Show: a two-seater sports model, a four-door open tourer and a four-door saloon. The robust chassis were available in two lengths, and the engines were Renwick and Bertelli's 1½-litre unit.

Harry Bertelli's coachbuilding business built the bodies. The new models were gradually put into production and about fourteen of the original design were made in the company's first two years.

Bert Bertelli had participated in competitive motoring events early in his career. He believed that the recent lack of such activity by Aston Martin was hampering sales as well as curtailing development. He persuaded the directors that the Le Mans 24 Hours race would be the best place to start redressing this. Two Team cars were built for the 1928 event, using a new dry sump version of the engine; both retired, but one of them won a prize for being the fastest 1½-litre car for the first twenty laps.

The company exhibited at the 1928 Olympia Motor Show, promoting Aston Martin as a 'Pleasure Car' as it was a pleasure both to drive and be driven in one. The cars were fitted with a new winged radiator badge. One of the Team cars was used as a demonstration vehicle and was the first Aston Martin to be road tested by *The Autocar*. However, by the end of the year only fourteen cars had been sold – in spite of its racing activity, economic conditions meant that selling expensive cars was not easy at this time, and the company faced financial difficulties.

One of the two Team cars built for the 1928 Le Mans 24 Hours race. This is chassis LM1 in racing trim with special mudguards and high mounted headlamps. The car was later used as a demonstrator.

An enterprising racing programme was pursued in 1929 to publicise the marque, including entries at Brooklands and in the Irish Grand Prix, but this did little to improve things and by September Aston Martin Motors faced bankruptcy. The company's rescuers were the garage proprietor S. C. Whitehouse, Percy Kidner (formerly the managing director of Vauxhall) and some other backers. The company was renamed Aston Martin Ltd and at this point the Charnwood financial connection ended.

The same year the International model was introduced at the London Motor Show; it used a dry sump version of the engine producing 56 bhp and two chassis lengths were available. The International was very successful and times seemed to be improving as just over 100 were sold in the next two years – a significant increase. Several body styles were available with the open 2/4-seater being the most popular. One-off cars were built too, such as the stylish coupé for W. S. Headlam in 1930.

It was agreed that racing would continue, and a new car based on the road vehicles was built. Good results were achieved at Brooklands and in the Irish GP. Improvements were made to the production cars, of which about sixty were built in 1930. The workforce numbered around forty-five, but by Christmas many had been laid off as the company again faced financial woes. The board of directors was rearranged, and William Renwick left the company. Bertelli's friend

This 1930 International has a unique coupé body designed and made for W. S. Headlam; the car still exists today. An International 2/4-seater is in the background.

A 1934 Mk II
long chassis
Sports Saloon.

H. J. Aldington of Frazer Nash provided vital credit guarantees which enabled the company to survive.

In spite of these difficulties three new Team cars based on the road-going International were built for the 1931 racing season. The three raced in the Brooklands Double Twelve, the Le Mans 24 Hours and the TT, achieving a class win each time.

Lance Prideaux-Brune, whose garage business needed a new make of car to sell, put some new capital into Aston Martin in the middle of the year and became a director of the company. The distribution and sale of the cars were handled by some new dealers, while the model range was widened to include near replicas of the Team cars. At the Olympia Motor Show there were new models including a four-door saloon and a drop-head coupé. Just over thirty cars were built in 1931.

The design of the cars was modified for 1932 to reduce costs by using proprietary gearboxes and axles. These are known as the Second Series cars and include the New International, Standard and Le Mans models. Various styles of open and closed bodies were available on two chassis lengths, and the enamel wings badge was introduced. Aston Martin won its class and the Rudge Whitworth cup at Le Mans in 1932 with Team cars again developed from the road vehicles. About 130 Second Series cars were made in two years.

Financial problems threatened the company late in 1932, and ownership passed from Prideaux-Brune to Sir Arthur

A sales leaflet for the 1934 Ulster; each car was guaranteed to achieve 100 mph.

The NEW "ULSTER" Model ASTON-MARTIN

● Guaranteed Maximum Speed 100 M.P.H.

● A Replica of the three cars which ran so successfully in the 1934 T.T. Race, finishing 3rd, 6th and 7th, and winning the TEAM PRIZE.

● Also making a new lap record of 77.4 m.p.h. in Class F.

To own one of these "ULSTER" MODEL ASTON-MARTINS is to experience "the real thing" in road racing, and to achieve higher average speeds and more consistent successes than ever before.
Moreover, they are built for durability with such precision that they hold their tune and maintain their performance with remarkable regularity.

Sutherland whose son, Gordon, became joint MD with Bert Bertelli. The new regime exercised closer financial control than previously and the fresh capital helped the development of new models.

The Third Series vehicles were in production in 1934 and 1935; they are also known as the Mk II. The models were developed from the earlier cars; the Standard model was dropped due to poor sales. Road-going versions of the Team cars, the Ulster, were sold for race or road use. The range included two chassis lengths; the 1½-litre engine now produced 73 bhp, with 85 bhp for the Ulster. A total of 165 Mk II road cars were built.

Racing continued using the Ulster Team cars, which were the last to race with the 1½-litre engine. At Le Mans in 1935 there were three Team cars and four works-supported private entries. The result was third overall, another class win, and the Rudge Whitworth cup. Later in the year Aston Martin won the Team prize in the TT race, repeating the 1934 result. From late 1934 the Team cars were painted red instead of green. In 1935 the Aston Martin Owners Club (AMOC) was established.

Sales were insufficient, perhaps because of high prices and the need for a more powerful engine. The 1½-litre unit was developed to 2 litres and produced 85 or 98 bhp; a new chassis was introduced with hydraulically operated brakes for the Speed Models. The Two-Litre and 15/98 were introduced in 1936 and produced until 1939. The costly competition programme was severely curtailed and the emphasis was more on excellent touring cars than high performance models, and a further action to promote sales was taken – the prices were reduced. Differences between Gordon Sutherland and Bert Bertelli led to the latter's leaving in 1937. Some Speed Model chassis were fitted with innovative streamlined bodies and sold as the Type C. Production of the Two-Litre range totalled 173.

Claude Hill, originally employed by Bert Bertelli in 1924, was now the chief designer and developed an advanced prototype ('The Atom') which eventually used a new 2-litre pushrod engine which he also designed.

A total of 678 cars were built between 1913 and 1940. During the Second World War the company made aircraft parts. In 1947 Sir Arthur Sutherland offered the company for sale. David Brown saw the advertisement and, after driving The Atom, decided to buy Aston Martin.

A 1938 Type C Speed Model is on the left, while on the right is the unique 1940 prototype known as 'The Atom'.

LE MANS

Sweeping triumph for
DAVID BROWN

By Appointment
His Royal Highness the Duke
Motor Car Manufac...
Aston Martin Lagond...

1ST ASTON MARTIN

R. SALVADORI — C. SHELBY *(Ave. 112.5 m.p.h.—2701 miles—New 3-litre records)*

2ND ASTON MARTIN

M. TRINTIGNAN — P. FRERE

*Subject to
Official Confirm...*

ASTON MARTIN LAGONDA LIMITED
A David Brown Company · Hanworth Park · Feltham · Middlesex   Telephone: FELtham 3641
London Showrooms: 96/97 Piccadilly London W.I.   Telephone: GROsvenor 7747
London Distributors: Brooklands of Bond Street Ltd W.I.   Telephone: MAYfair 8351

DAVID BROWN: 1947–72

Shortly after buying Aston Martin, David Brown purchased the Lagonda Company, which had developed a promising six-cylinder engine and a new chassis designed under the guidance of W. O. Bentley. With a 2.6-litre engine, the Lagonda went into production in 1949, using engines and gearboxes produced at the David Brown factory in Melham, Yorkshire. The car was available as a drop-head coupé or four-door saloon. Production finished in 1954, by which time about 550 had been built.

David Brown based Aston Martin Ltd at Hanworth, west of London, near Feltham. Like his predecessors, he believed in the value of competition and was persuaded to enter a car for the 1948 Spa 24 Hours race. Built in just nine weeks the open-bodied car used Claude Hill's Atom chassis and engine; it won the race. A road version called the Two-Litre Sports (retrospectively named the DB1, using David Brown's initials) went into production and fifteen were sold. The design evolved into the three DB2 saloons made in 1949 which were development vehicles for racing rather than prototypes for the road cars. Five more racing DB2s were built. Results included

Opposite: After many years of effort Aston Martin won the Le Mans 24 hours race in 1959. The result was advertised widely.

The badge used on cars in the David Brown years. The usual finish was chromium but this gold-plated version was used on some cars.

The Two-Litre Sports (DB1) with a 2.6-litre Lagonda behind it. THX 231 was the first car of the David Brown era to be sold.

An early DB2 with the three-piece grille and air vents behind the front wheels. After the construction of about fifty cars the design was altered and subsequent DB2s were built with a one-piece grille and no air vents in the body sides.

third in the 1950 Ulster TT, and class wins at Le Mans in 1950 and 1951. Good finishes were also achieved in the Alpine Rally and the Mille Miglia. The winged Aston Martin badge had 'David Brown' added in 1949.

The DB2 design was refined and put into production in mid 1950. The car used the Lagonda six-cylinder, twin ohc engine which produced 105 bhp, or 125 bhp in Vantage tune. The term Vantage was subsequently used for cars with engines producing more power than the standard models. The car had a two-seater saloon body, and the grille was similar to the pre-1940 radiator with an additional small vent each side; these were later combined into a single grille. An open drop-head version was introduced later the same year. The DB2 was in production for three years and 410 were made.

In 1950 John Wyer joined the company for one year to run the racing team; he stayed until 1963. It became

clear that using modified road cars in top-class racing would produce limited success, so Aston Martin recruited Austrian engineer Robert Eberan von Eberhorst to design a car specifically for competition. The car used the 2.6-litre engine developed to produce 140 bhp. The first of these open DB3 cars took part in the Ulster TT in September 1951, but it retired. The best result was to win the 1952 Goodwood Nine Hours race driven by Peter Collins and Pat Griffith; in this event another DB3 caught fire in the pits. Ten DB3s were built, five were Team cars and five sold to customers. The DB3 did not perform as well as hoped and work on a replacement started late in 1952.

The new racing-car chassis was designed by Willie Watson; it was smaller and lighter than its predecessor and the car was – for many people – better looking. The cars initially had a 182 bhp version of the 3-litre engine; the output was eventually 240 bhp. The prototype DB3S was tested early in 1953 and the type was the company's main competition car for the next four years, during which time it was continually improved and developed. Eleven Team cars and twenty customer cars

John Wyer joined Aston Martin for one year to manage the racing team but instead stayed for thirteen years and became General Manager.

The 1951 DB3 racing car chassis designed by Robert Eberan von Eberhorst.

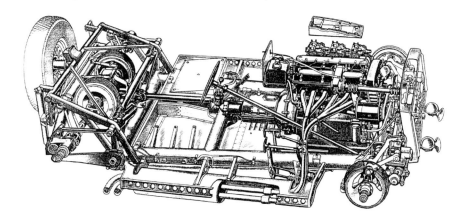

Sebring, Florida,
March 1954:
three DB3S
Team cars (in
the earliest form
of the car) are
prepared for the
12 Hours race,
during which all
three retired.

Sebring, Florida, March 1954: three DB3S Team cars (in the earliest form of the car) are prepared for the 12 Hours race, during which all three retired.

were made. Some of the best results were at Le Mans where a DB3S came second in 1955, 1956 and 1958.

In 1953 Lagonda revised its range with the introduction of a 3-litre version of the engine and new bodywork designed by Tickford of Newport Pagnell. The new cars were available as a two-door saloon or two-door drop-head coupé, with a four-door saloon introduced the following year. The cars were manufactured until 1958, by which time 244 had been produced.

The DB2 was well received when it first went on sale, but it was felt that with two rear seats it would be even more successful. The result was the DB2/4, announced in 1953 in both saloon and drop-head versions. The rear seat backs could be folded down and the saloon had a large opening rear panel – the first hatchback. The engine was enlarged to 3 litres from 1953. Production was now concentrated at Feltham. The DB2/4 Mk II was produced from 1955 to 1957; it had slightly revised bodywork and interior. A total of 761 DB2/4 and Mk II were built.

In order to have a more competitive racing car a V12 version of the engine was developed and appeared in new cars in 1954; known as the Lagonda V12s they looked like enlarged DB3Ss. Four were built but technical difficulties

A 1954 DB2/4 drop-head coupé. The amber lamps under the rear bumper are not original.

resulted in the closure of the programme the following year. Two of them appeared in the 1956 film *Checkpoint*.

David Brown bought Tickford of Newport Pagnell in 1955 and, as a result, all Aston Martin and Lagonda production was moved there. Following the established practice, a service department was opened near the factory.

The final development of cars using the Claude Hill chassis was the DB Mk III which was announced in 1957 and remained in production until 1959; 552 were made. The cars were available in saloon and drop-head versions; in addition five fixed-head coupés were made. The grille was modified to resemble that of the DB3S and the instruments were grouped behind the steering wheel. Disc brakes were available. A small number of the Claude Hill chassis were supplied to coachbuilders such as Bertone and Touring for special bodies.

Racing activity continued energetically, and in 1956 the completely new prototype DBR1 designed by Ted Cutting went to Le Mans for its first event. It retired in the twenty-first hour – an excellent debut. In 1959 a development of the car won the race driven by Roy Salvadori and Carroll Shelby, another DBR1 was second, and the third one driven by Stirling Moss and Jack Fairman retired after having led the race. A final win in the Goodwood Nine Hours race

Above: The Le Mans 24 Hours race, June 1959. The winning DBR1 passes the grandstands.

Above right: Celebrating the 1959 Le Mans win; Reg Parnell, the team manager, is on the left, with drivers Carroll Shelby (in the centre with the trophy) and Roy Salvadori.

Opposite: The DB4GT with shortened chassis, faired headlamps and uprated engine.

(during which a DBR1 caught fire in the pits) secured the World Sports Car Championship for Aston Martin in 1959. Five DBR1s were built with a few additional variants; the engines were either 2½- or 3-litre capacity, depending upon the racing regulations. The DBR1 programme ceased after AML won the Championship.

In addition to sports-car racing David Brown wanted to compete in Formula 1. Design of the DBR4 started in 1955, at the same time as for the DBR1, and they had much in common. The prototype was tested in December 1957 but work was suspended for most of the following year to focus effort on the DBR1. The F1 car was announced publicly in April 1959, and two were entered for their first event in the International Trophy race at Silverstone; Roy Salvadori finished second and Carroll Shelby retired on the last lap. The change to rear engines by other Formula 1 manufacturers and delayed development had combined to make the Aston Martins uncompetitive, and the Silverstone result was the best that the factory achieved. The company withdrew from F1 after the 1960 season.

Interest in Aston Martin's road cars increased considerably in late 1958 with the introduction of the four-seater DB4 Coupé. The bodies of these new cars were designed by Touring of Milan, and built using that company's Superleggera system

with a framework of narrow tubes covered by hand-beaten aluminium body panels. The platform chassis was designed by Harold Beach, and the 3.7-litre six-cylinder engine, producing 240 bhp, by Tadek Marek. The convertible version was introduced in 1961. The DB4 was in production until 1963 and was regularly updated. A total of 1,110 were built.

A short wheelbase two-seater DB4GT was introduced at the 1959 London Motor Show with an increased power output and faired headlamps. Before the launch the prototype raced at Silverstone when Stirling Moss won his event at the BRDC meeting and set the lap record; the same car retired in the Le Mans 24 Hours race later in the year. Production of the

Above: The development of the design is shown with the 1958 DB Mk III on the left, an experimental car which used DB Mk III and DB4 parts in the centre, and on the right a late Series 4 DB4 of 1962.

A DB4GT Zagato Sanction II.

DB4GT finished in 1963 by which time seventy-five had been built.

In 1960 the DB4GT was offered with a lightweight body by Carrozzeria Zagato; for many people this is the best-looking of the DB Aston Martins. These cars were intended for racing or for the road. The chassis were shipped to Milan for the bodywork to be fitted. Zagato made bodies for twenty cars. In 1991 a further four DB4GT Zagatos were completed with full factory approval; these were made by R. S. Williams and are known as the Sanction II cars; two final ones (Sanction III) were built in 2000.

In 1961 the Lagonda name was revived with the introduction of the Rapide. The new car was based on the DB4 using a longer chassis and de Dion rear suspension; the engine was enlarged to 4 litres. Most had automatic transmission. The styling was undertaken by Touring and had some similarities with the DB4 although it had four doors and a unique front. The interior was

A Lagonda Rapide; this model is the forty-seventh of the fifty-five cars made in total.

luxuriously appointed. The total production over three years was fifty-five cars; most were built to order which resulted in small specification variations.

The company's withdrawal from international motor racing disappointed many of the dealers who strongly believed that involvement in competition helped sell road cars. As a result the factory changed its mind and some new racers were developed from the DB4GT and these are known as the Project cars. The first (Project 212) raced at Le Mans in 1962. The following year three new cars (two Project 214s and one Project 215) ran at Le Mans; all three retired. One of the final races for these Team cars was the Inter-Europa Cup at Monza in 1963 in which a Project 214 competed; driven by Roy Salvadori, it won the race.

Project 215, driven by Phil Hill and Lucien Bianchi at Le Mans, 1963.

The development of the road cars continued in parallel with the racing activity. Following the success of the DB4 the DB5 was announced in 1963; it was available as a saloon and convertible. The main visual change was the faired headlamps first seen on the DB4GT. The engine was enlarged to 4 litres and produced 282 bhp. The DB5 became famous when driven by James Bond in the film *Goldfinger*. Production of the DB5 was 1,022, including a dozen converted into shooting brakes.

The wheelbase of the DB5 was lengthened in 1965, providing more rear space, and the resulting car given a vertical Kamm tail similar to that used on the later Project cars to produce the DB6. The convertible version, called the Volante, was announced at the same time, and the name has been used for all open cars since, including production current at the time of writing. The DB6 Mk 2 was introduced in 1969. Sharing some components with the forthcoming DBS and with flared wheel arches, it was the final development of

Overleaf: A works demonstration DB6 Mk 2 Volante, 1969.

the DB4. The DB6 Mk 2 Volante belonging to HRH Prince Charles was used by the Duke and Duchess of Cambridge after their wedding in 2011. The total production of the DB6 was 1,751 cars when production ended in 1970.

A new model was planned using the expertise of Touring of Milan who had worked successfully on the DB4. The car was to be a two-door, two-seater coupé based on the DB6. Two prototypes, known as the DBSC, were ready in late 1966, but Touring was in receivership and no further cars were built.

Tadek Marek had begun work in 1963 on a V8 engine to replace the six-cylinder unit, using common parts where possible. The first unit ran two years later. The engine was publicly announced in January 1967 and two Lola T70s raced at Le Mans later that year, powered by the new 5-litre V8; however, both cars retired with engine failure and further development was undertaken, leading to further delays in the V8 engine's production.

In October 1967 the DBS was introduced, designed by William Towns: a two-door, four-seater coupé (with no Volante version). This striking-looking car used many of the mechanical parts from the DB6. It had wire wheels, four headlamps and a full-width grille echoing those from earlier models. The DBS should have used the new V8 engine, but as it was not ready it was launched with the six-cylinder unit. The V8 engine, now 5.3 litres, was ready in 1969, and the DBS V8 was introduced in October. Production of the six-cylinder DBS and the DB6 Mk II continued. The DBS V8 had a spoiler under the front bumper and alloy wheels, but otherwise looked much like the earlier car. A total of 786 six-cylinder DBSs and 400 of the V8s were built before production ended in 1972.

David Brown wanted a replacement for the Lagonda Rapide, and a four-door prototype based on the DBS was revealed at the start of 1970. It had the four headlamps and grille from the DBS, but Lagonda badges. Work on the project was interrupted as a result of the sale of the company shortly afterwards.

Aston Martin had never really been a profitable enterprise for Sir David Brown (knighted in 1968) and so in 1972 it was sold to Company Developments, a Midlands-based investment company. During the DB years the company made just over 7,000 cars.

The DBS was introduced in 1967. This car was built in 1970 with the Vantage engine.

EXCELLENCE

It is a wretched taste to be gratified with mediocrity
when the excellent lies before us.

ISAAC D'ISRAELI

1766-1848

For details of the ultimate in motoring, "The Aston Martin Experience," contact: Victor Gauntlett, Executive Ch
Aston Martin Lagonda Ltd., Tickford Street, Newport Pagnell, Buckinghamshire, MK16 9AN
Telephone: Newport Pagnell (0908) 610620, or your Aston Martin Lagonda Distributor, for personal atten

CHANGING OWNERSHIP: 1972–87

Aston Martin Lagonda Ltd's new chairman, S. William Willson, believed that it could raise profitability by improving efficiency and abandoning racing. One initial action was to remove DB from the names. A little later the fronts of the cars were changed to incorporate two headlamps and a revised grille – although still with the traditional shape. The six-cylinder models were renamed the AM Vantage, a somewhat confusing use of the name; production finished after a year.

The 1972 cars with the V8 engine were renamed Aston Martin V8 and remained in production until 1989.

Opposite: This is one of a series of advertisements used in 1981–2. It shows well the range of V8-engined cars available.

An early Aston Martin V8, showing its alloy wheels.

During this time several identifiable versions were built. The first lasted a year and introduced the two headlamps and new grille. The next change came in 1973 when the V8 engines were fitted with Weber carburettors and the bonnet had a higher air intake.

It was decided that the 1970 four-door DBS prototype should be developed, and in October 1974 the new model was announced. Powered by the V8 engine, it had a revised front with two headlamps and a grille reminiscent of the Rapide, and was named the Aston Martin Lagonda. Seven cars had been completed when production ended in 1976.

In 1974 the company was again in financial trouble. Economic times were hard and selling cars was difficult. A receiver was appointed, and the factory closed in December after having produced 720 vehicles in two years. The service department continued operations.

Left to right: Fred Hartley (sales); Peter Sprague; Eric Harmer; Denis Flather; Alan Curtis; and George Minden. Eric Harmer sent his pocket money to help save AML when it was in receivership and was a guest of the directors at Newport Pagnell in April 1976.

The company was rescued by George Minden, Peter Sprague, Alan Curtis and Denis Flather, and renamed Aston Martin Lagonda (1975) Ltd. Production restarted in 1976 and reached nearly six cars a week; there was little change to the specifications of the V8 and Lagonda.

A 1976 V8 Lagonda with its distinctive styling.

Late that year a completely new four-door V8 Lagonda designed by William Towns was announced. It was a spectacular departure from previous models with its wedge-shaped body and advanced electronics; it attracted enormous attention – and numerous orders. Much development was needed to get the car into production; the first was delivered in April 1978. By the time the Lagonda was discontinued in 1989 a total of 636 cars had been made.

Early in 1977 the V8 Vantage was announced. Its revised engine produced substantially more power than the standard unit. The visual changes included the blanked-off grille which

An Oscar India V8 saloon with the reshaped bonnet bulge, 1978.

had two additional lamps, closure of the bonnet air intake and a deep air dam below the bumper; at the rear there was a full-width spoiler. The 1981 *Motor* road test found it to be the fastest standard production car ever tested, with a maximum speed of nearly 170 mph.

The company was, according to Engineering Director Michael Bowler, sympathetic to returning to racing but lacked a suitable vehicle. An enthusiastic dealer called Robin Hamilton developed a V8 into a competent racing car with some unofficial factory help; it finished seventeenth in the 1977 Le Mans 24 Hours race. In 1979 it raced again but retired.

The next versions of the V8 and V8 Vantage came in October 1978 and are known as the Oscar India (for 'October Introduction') models. The most noticeable changes were to the bonnet with its closed air intake and reshaped bulge, plus a neatly incorporated full-width rear spoiler. The V8 interior was given wood trim panels. Detailed improvements continued to be made to the cars, but, with the V8 costing £27,000 and the Lagonda £37,500, the economic climate made sales difficult. In 1979 the company sold seventy-four cars, including thirty-three Lagondas.

There was no convertible car in the range from 1970 until the V8 Volante was announced in 1978. Designed by Harold Beach, it featured the Oscar India bonnet and wood trim, and had a power-operated folding hood. Much early production went to the USA.

In April 1980 the company revealed a mid-engined two-seater with a turbocharged engine and gullwing doors. With individualistic styling by William Towns, this unique car (named Bulldog) was intended to publicise the availability of AML expertise to the motor

Victor Gauntlett, sitting in one of the 1922 Grand Prix cars, later known as Green Pea.

industry. Work was subsequently undertaken on the Ford Capri, the Jaguar XJS, the Tickford Metro and AML's V8 race engine. Much of this was done by Aston Martin Tickford, the wholly owned subsidiary in Milton Keynes.

Further changes in the company's shareholders occurred in 1980 with the addition of CH Industrials Ltd and Pace Petroleum, whose founder was Victor Gauntlett. At the end of 1980 these two bought out the other shareholders, George Minden having left in 1978. The company was renamed Aston Martin Lagonda Ltd. Victor Gauntlett became the chief executive and joint chairman with Tim Hearley, the chairman of CH Industrials.

Robin Hamilton, encouraged by his results with the V8 Vantage, approached AML about a return to racing. The result was Nimrod Racing Automobiles, partly funded by Pace Petroleum and AML, with V8 engines from AM Tickford.

A Vantage Volante showing the extended sills and wheel arches. The wheels were not usually painted the same colour as the body.

The cars first raced in 1982, and one of the best results was achieved at Le Mans that year when one car finished seventh overall and fourth in class; Nimrod also came third in the 1982 World Sports Car Championship. Five cars were built: four to Group C regulations and one to the North American IMSA specification. The programme ran for three years and included events in the USA, the UK and Europe.

Pace Petroleum was taken over in 1983 and its shareholding in Aston Martin was sold to Automotive Investments Inc., which was owned by the Papanicolaou and Livanos families. Victor Gauntlett remained as Chairman. Soon afterwards Automotive Investments Inc. took control of AML and strengthened its engineering abilities.

In April 1984 the 10,000th Aston Martin, a red V8, was revealed at Newport Pagnell. Later in the year the Livanos family took a 75 per cent interest in the company, with Victor Gauntlett having the remainder.

Two years later a Vantage version of the V8 Volante was announced. New features included extended wheel arches, sills and rear spoiler as well as the more powerful engine.

Prince Charles had a special version with understated body changes; about another twenty-five were built and are known as the Prince of Wales (P of W) specification Vantage Volantes.

At the beginning of 1986 the V8 engines were fitted with electronic fuel injection to increase power and efficiency. The result was a much lower bonnet bulge without an air intake. Later in the year the V8 Vantage Zagato went on sale; this was a two-door, two-seater, with bodywork designed and constructed by Zagato. By 1988 a total of fifty-two had been made. The maximum speed was about 186 mph. Demand for an open version resulted in thirty-seven Volantes being built on the V8 mechanical components in 1987 and 1988; a few were fitted with the more powerful Vantage engine.

Production of the Towns-designed V8 range finished in 1989. Work had begun on a replacement late in 1985, and the new Virage was launched while AML was under Ford ownership.

A V8 Zagato Volante in front of a V8 Vantage Zagato.

FORD MOTOR COMPANY: 1987–2007

VICTOR GAUNTLETT SAW that the company would have difficulty continuing as an independent organisation; under his guidance and with the enthusiastic support of Walter Hayes (then vice chairman of Ford Europe) the Ford Motor Company bought a controlling interest in 1987. Ford let Aston Martin develop without undue interference and gave it the financial and technical backing that it so urgently needed. Walter Hayes was chairman of AML from 1987 to 1994, and was the original chairman of the Aston Martin Heritage Trust (AMHT) when it was founded in 1998.

In 1987 Aston Martin announced its return to top-class international motor racing. Proteus Technology Ltd was formed and unveiled the AMR1 late the following year. The design by Max Boxtrom was new and the engine was based on the four-valve V8 unit being developed for the forthcoming Virage. Five cars were built and four of them raced in the World Sports-Prototype Championship Group C series in 1989. The best result was at Brands Hatch, when David Leslie and Brian Redman finished fourth. At Le Mans one of the AMR1s (which now belongs to the AMHT) finished eleventh and the other retired. The AMR1 programme stopped at the end of the year; the team had come sixth in the Championship.

The first all new road car produced under Ford ownership was the Virage, launched in 1988. The car used a version of the 1969 V8 engine, producing 330 bhp, and was the last

In 1990, nine different V8-engined cars were commissioned to celebrate twenty-one years of V8 production. The cars were finished in Hunter green paint, tan leather, burr walnut veneer trim and dark green carpet. They are known as the Hunter Collection. The central five cars are, from the left: Oscar India saloon; Vantage Oscar India Volante P of W specification; Virage saloon; Oscar India Volante; Vantage Oscar India saloon.

model range to have a handmade aluminium body. Some of the chassis components were developed from those used on the final Lagondas. The Virage was a two-door, four-seater, in coupé and open versions. Later models were called V8 Coupés and dropped the Virage name. An overall total of 1,060 Virage-based cars were built.

The interior of a V8 Coupé of the late 1990s.

The fifth AMR1 to be built, shown in the Donington Park 300-mile race in September 1989. It finished seventh and was driven by Brian Redman and David Sears.

Works Service offered a 6.3-litre conversion on the standard 5.3-litre Virage in 1992. AML introduced the Virage Vantage in 1994 with a supercharged 5.3-litre engine producing 550 bhp; it was in production until 1999. Works Service then developed a 600-bhp version of the supercharged Vantage. A special version known as the Vantage Le Mans was made in 1999 to commemorate the 1959 Le Mans win. A total of 280 Vantages were produced.

The Virage Volante was introduced in 1992 and 234 were made during its four-and-a-half-year production, plus sixty-three on a lengthened wheelbase. Additional Virage-derived models included shooting brakes, Limited Edition Coupés

The 1998 Vantage V600, a high-performance conversion by Works Service. It was one of the most powerful of the Virage-derived cars.

and the Vantage Volante Special Edition. Production of these cars continued at Newport Pagnell until 2000.

Victor Gauntlett had long believed that a less expensive car was needed for AML to survive. It was not until Ford took control that the plan was implemented. The new car, the two-plus-two DB7 Coupé (whose name revived the link with David Brown), was unveiled in 1994 and was the first 'high volume' Aston Martin. The design was by Ian Callum. The cars were built at Bloxham, Oxfordshire and were the first of the company's cars to make extensive use of composite materials and some new manufacturing technology. The engine was a 3.2-litre, six-cylinder, supercharged unit. The coupé was joined two years later by a Volante. The V12-engined DB7 Vantage replaced the

The three-door Virage shooting brake; two were built in 1992.

Walter Hayes
(on the left)
with Sir David
Brown (then
life President
of AML) and an
early six-cylinder
DB7 Coupé.

six-cylinder car in 1999 and remained in production until late 2003. The total production of all DB7s was just under 7,100 in nine years – an enormous increase for AML.

During its life several models were derived from the DB7. Most were limited editions made for particular dealers or events. The DB7 GT with uprated engine was introduced in late 2002. The Zagato connection was renewed in 2003 with a special-bodied version of the Vantage Coupé. An open version, the DB AR1, was made for the North-American market in 2003 – it was based on the DB7 Zagato but

The DB7 Vantage
Volante, showing
the revised front
lamps.

had neither hood nor rear seats, and all but one of the 100 produced were left-hand drive.

A prototype called Project Vantage was revealed in 1998 and was the forerunner of the next major model, the V12 Vanquish. This was the first Aston Martin to use new technology such as aluminium extrusions and carbon fibre, and construction methods including bonding instead of bolts and rivets. The V12 Vanquish was launched in 2001, the year after the new CEO, Dr Ulrich Bez, joined AML. The cars were powered by the six-litre V12 engine first seen in the DB7 Vantage and which was to be one of the main power units used by the company for several years. The specification was uprated in 2004 with a more powerful engine, improved suspension and revised bodywork; it continued in this form until production ceased in 2007 with the V12 Vanquish S Ultimate Edition. Just over 2,500 V12 Vanquishes were built; unusually AML did not make a convertible version. These were the last cars to be manufactured at Newport Pagnell.

The all-new two-door DB9 Coupé started in production in January 2004 and was a turning point in AML's history, even though this was not marked by a change in ownership; it pioneered the use of VH ('vertical and horizontal') architecture, which is a unique engineering philosophy developed by

The 2001 V12 Vanquish: the last model made at Newport Pagnell.

The 4.3-litre V8 Vantage Roadster, 2007. The car is an early one which was used for publicity.

AML enabling different models to share major components. It was the first car designed under the leadership of Dr Bez, making extensive use of aluminium. It was the first model to be built at Aston Martin's new Gaydon factory. The DB9 used a revised 450-bhp version of the six-litre V12 engine, and a rear-mounted six-speed manual or automatic transaxle. The DB9 Volante was introduced in February 2005. Improvements were made to the specification each year, the most major being in 2012, and some limited edition models were made. The DB9 remains in production and can be seen as the beginning of the modern era for AML, even though the company remained in Ford ownership for a few more years.

The company decided that the policy 'racing improves the breed' would again be followed. A new company, Aston Martin Racing, was formed in 2003 to design and build Aston Martin racing cars. It was a joint venture between AML and Prodrive, a world-class motorsport and automotive technology company. The new vehicles were developed from the DB9 Coupé. The first event for the DBR9 racing car was at Sebring in early 2005 where it won the GT1 class. Further entries and success around the world followed this initial result, and included winning the GT1 class in the Le Mans 24 Hours race in 2007 and again in 2008, by which time the cars sported the light blue and orange colours of their Gulf sponsors. Similar cars sold to customers, as has been Aston Martin practice, also produced good results. Ten Team cars and nine customer cars were built by the time production finished in 2009. A less powerful version, the DBRS9, was built to meet GT3 regulations and was produced from

2005 to 2010. These were designed for club racing and track days; in total twenty-seven cars were built.

The 2005 Geneva Motor Show was used to unveil the new two-

door, hatchback-bodied, two-seater V8 Vantage which had a 4.3-litre engine and a rear-mounted six-speed transaxle. It was in production until the 4.7-litre engine was introduced in 2008. This model was to play an important role in AML's future as many derivatives were developed. The first was the racing V8 Vantage N24 which was introduced at the Nürburgring 24 Hours race in June 2006 and designed for events such as the European GT4 series. Fifty-three N24s were built before production stopped in 2008. An open version called the V8 Vantage Roadster was introduced in spring 2007; this was mechanically similar to the coupé. Later the same year Ford's financial difficulties forced it to sell AML, and the company again needed a new backer.

Le Mans, 2006. This DBR9, driven by Stephane Sarrazin, Pedro Lamy and Stephane Ortelli finished tenth overall and fifth in its class.

The DB9 was introduced in 2004 and was the first model built at Gaydon.

THE MODERN ERA: 2007–13

THE COMPANY WAS bought by an investment consortium, mainly from Kuwait, under the chairmanship of David Richards, the chairman of Prodrive, with Ulrich Bez remaining the CEO. Dr Bez's influence is shown both in the return to racing with the DBR9, and in the development of the road cars using the V8 and V12 engines. Continuity of the models in production was maintained.

In July 2007 V12 Vanquish production finished at Newport Pagnell and the factory closed, although Works Service remained; production was now exclusively at Gaydon. A new model was announced in August: the DBS with the familiar V12 engine now producing 510 bhp; for the first time carbon fibre was used for some of the body panels. It was developed from the DB9 and used VH architecture. The DBS was initially a two-seater; rear seats soon became options. The convertible Volante version was introduced in 2009. Production finished in 2012 by which time 2,533 coupés and 852 Volantes had been built.

Development of the successful V8 Vantage continued with the engine being enlarged to 4.7 litres for both coupé and roadster in May 2008; later the same year production of the V8 Vantage reached 10,000 cars. In 2011 the V8 Vantage S was announced with an uprated engine, seven-speed transaxle and improved aerodynamics. More racing versions became available in 2008 with the V8 Vantage GT2 in January and the 4.7-litre GT4 replacing the N24 in November. At this time AML could supply cars for all four GT classes.

The Virage name, first used in 1988, was given to this car, which was in production from spring 2011 until autumn the following year.

David Richards (on the left) and Dr Ulrich Bez outside the Gaydon factory.

AML's entries in the top class of racing switched from the DBR9 to the Lola-Aston Martin LMP1 in 2009 and 2010; these closed cars used the 6-litre V12 engine. At Le Mans in 2009 one car finished fourth overall and was the first petrol-powered car behind the diesel-engined Audis. The replacement for 2011 was the all-new AMR-One, an open car with a specially designed petrol engine; however, it had reliability problems at Le Mans and did not race again.

A new four-door, four-seater sports car called the Rapide was introduced early in 2010. The Gaydon factory was at full capacity, and initial production was by Magna Steyr in Austria; this was later transferred to Gaydon. The Rapide was based on a lengthened DB9 and had folding rear seats and a tailgate. The engine was a 470-bhp version of the 6-litre V12 unit. In May 2010 a Rapide came second in its class at the Nürburgring 24 Hours race. Three years later the Rapide S was announced with a restyled front and numerous other improvements. Later in the year a hydrogen-powered Rapide raced at the Nürburgring. The Rapide S remains in production.

The 2007 DBS, the 'flagship' of the range.

A new version of the Vantage went into production in April 2009, having been announced a year earlier. It had

A V12 Vantage factory demonstrator, 2009.

the 6-litre V12 engine which produced 510 bhp. The V12 Vantage Coupé, like the V8 version, uses VH architecture. The main external features are extra air vents on the bonnet and a rear spoiler. A racing version soon appeared and won its class in the 2009 Nürburgring 24 Hours race. In May 2011 a Zagato-bodied version of the V12 Vantage was announced; two prototypes raced at the Nürburgring, one winning the class. Production of the V12 Vantage Zagato was limited to 101 cars, but the V12 Vantage coupé remains in production.

The One-77 hypercar went into production at Gaydon late in 2010, following the gradual release of information to the media; production was limited to seventy-seven cars and deliveries started the following year. The cars had a carbon fibre monocoque and aluminium body panels; the 7.3-litre V12 engine was front-mounted and produced 750 bhp; and the top speed was 220 mph. Every aspect of the One-77 was state

The 2011 V12 Vantage Zagato.

Two One-77s being built in a special section of the Gaydon factory.

of the art. The UK price for a One-77 was about £1.2 million plus taxes; all were soon sold.

Buyers of the One-77 could choose from a wide range of options, and soon similar choices were available through the 'Q by Aston Martin' bespoke service for all new AML cars – the name was perhaps inspired by 'Q' in the James Bond films. A huge range of colours and materials was available for customers to tailor a car to their personal requirements – an approach that Aston Martin has used through much of its long history. In 2011 AML was proclaimed the 'Coolest Brand' for the fifth time, and in 2013 it came second.

AML introduced the Cygnet in 2011. This was a city car based on the Toyota IQ but with extensively revised bodywork and interior, all to Aston Martin's usual high standards, leaving the mechanical units unchanged. The wide two-door body gave roomy accommodation to the front passengers but rather less in the rear. Cygnets were produced at Gaydon until late 2013, by which time nearly 1,000 had been built.

The Cygnet; this car was shown at the 2010 Geneva Motor Show.

Another new model, announced early in 2011, was the V12 Virage, fitting between the DB9 and the

DBS. It was a two-door coupé available with either an additional two seats or a shelf at the rear. The open Volante version soon followed and was only available with two-plus-two seating. The Virage had a 489-bhp version of the 6-litre V12 engine and a rear-mounted six-speed transaxle. Production finished in October 2012 after 1,100 cars had been made.

In August 2012 the V12 Vantage Roadster was announced. This was essentially the V12 Vantage with a roadster body. Almost a year later a new version of the V12 Vantage Coupé was announced, the V12 Vantage S. This car is currently the fastest road-going Aston Martin, apart from the One-77, with a top speed of 205 mph. The revised engine produces 565 bhp. The seven-speed automated manual transaxle is controlled with paddles behind the steering wheel. The coupé and roadster versions of the Vantage remain in production. In parallel with the road cars, AML continues to produce competitive racing cars based on the V8 and V12 Vantage for the GT Pro and GT Am classes.

In mid 2012 a new car was announced using the name Vanquish; deliveries started in late 2012. It uses the latest version of Aston Martin's flexible VH architecture and has body panels formed from carbon fibre. The rear spoiler is an

The 2012 Vanquish.

integral part of the boot lid. The car has a revised 6-litre V12 engine producing 565 bhp, and in the most confident fashion marks 100 years of Aston Martin. In May 2013 the Vanquish Volante was announced with deliveries starting by the end of the year; mechanically it is the same as the coupé. An unusual feature is that the windscreen is full height so that the glass runs up to meet the folding roof.

By September 2012 the DB9 had been in production for over eight years, during which time it had received numerous specification enhancements. A series of major changes were then introduced, and these included improvements to the bodywork, uprating the engine power to 510 bhp, fitting a new six-speed automatic transaxle, and improved brakes and suspension. The revitalised DB9 remains in production.

Late in 2012 the Italian equity group Investindustrial purchased a 37.5 per cent stake in AML, thus providing some much-needed capital. The following year news emerged of a technical collaboration between AML and Mercedes-AMG. By December the two parties had signed an agreement for technical cooperation; Mercedes would receive non-voting shares in AML.

The CC100 Speedster.

In its centenary year AML announced an innovative concept car, the CC100 Speedster. It was not intended for

production, but as a celebration which looked back to the 1959 Le Mans-winning DBR1, and forward to future Aston Martins. The CC100 has an open carbon fibre body, no hood, two faired headrests and large cut-outs below the doors. It is fitted with the familiar 6-litre V12 engine and six-speed transaxle, and uses VH architecture. The car first appeared in May 2013 at the Nürburgring 24 Hours race meeting and the following month at Le Mans to mark AML's centenary. The design was directed by Marek Reichman.

The factory racing activity continued in 2013 and resulted in a win in the World Endurance Championship for the GTE Am team. At Le Mans one of the GTE Pro cars came third and a GTE Am car finished sixth.

Throughout 2013 events took place around the world to mark one hundred years of Aston Martin and the production of about 65,000 cars, most of which still exist. In July there was the timeline display of 101 cars in Kensington Gardens, London; AML published a special yearbook; the AMHT commissioned two model collections from SMTS; the AMOC organised numerous events. AML remains an iconic car manufacturer with an enthusiastic following around the world. The year 2013 was a memorable celebration of the centenary of a great car company.

The five Team cars at Le Mans in the pit lane, 2013.

JAMES BOND AND ASTON MARTIN

JAMES BOND ORIGINATED with Ian Fleming's novels. *Casino Royale* was the first of these and was published in 1953. The first Bond film was *Dr No*, released in 1962, four years after the book and the Aston Martin connection to the films was made in *Goldfinger* in 1964. The early Ian Fleming novels had James Bond driving a 1930s Bentley; later, in the seventh book, *Goldfinger*, there was an Aston Martin DB III (it should perhaps have been a DB Mk III), which had a few non-standard features including reinforced bumpers and stowage for a Colt .45 revolver.

The emphasis on the cars in the films increased with each one: Eon Productions wanted something dramatic to draw in the audience after their initial successes. The car in the first film *Dr No* was a Sunbeam Alpine, and in the next one *From Russia With Love* there was brief use of a 1935 Bentley. *Goldfinger* (1964) saw the debut of the now well-known silver Aston Martin DB5. But obtaining the DB5 had not been straightforward.

When Eon approached AML for a car the company, often receiving such requests, offered to sell one. Once it had seen the sort of special equipment which the film-makers had in mind for the car, AML felt that the changes were impossible and decided not to pursue the matter. Eon, however, wanted to use the make of car which Ian Fleming had specified. Eventually AML was persuaded that the publicity which would result from films would be worth the effort.

The car provided to Eon for *Goldfinger* was a works experimental vehicle; originally a DB4 Series 5 modified as a prototype DB5, it was a 1963 Earls Court Motor Show car. The film company made the necessary modifications to install the spectacular special equipment for the film. The best-known items are perhaps the passenger ejector seat, the revolving number plates and the tyre-slasher in the rear axle. This was known as the effects car, as opposed to the road car, which was another DB5 loaned by AML and modified for filming to look like the effects car.

When filming was completed the effects car was made roadworthy and shown at numerous events around the UK, gaining enormous publicity for the film, AML and Sean Connery. The car then went on an international tour

Sean Connery as James Bond and the DB5 from the 1964 film *Goldfinger*.

The control
panel in the DB5.

including North America, Japan and Europe. The demands
for the 007 DB5 were such that the road car was later fitted
with the same functioning gadgets as the effects car. AML
found it necessary to produce a leaflet and a press release
giving details of the car.

The 1965 film *Thunderball* featured the DB5 road car, and
Eon Productions ordered two DB5s with full 007 equipment
in order to promote it. These two are known as the show cars
and were initially for use in North America. A huge amount
of publicity was again generated. Aston Martin used its two
DB5s, the effects car and the road car, for its own PR purposes
when they were not needed by Eon.

In 1968 the effects car had its special equipment removed,
and it was returned to standard specification and sold as a
used car with a new registration number. AML retained the
original number BMT 216A. The new owner refitted many
of the 007 features, but without access to the original parts.
The car was then sold again and went to the USA; in June
1997 it was stolen and has not been seen since.

The road car was sold to a private owner in 1969 and retained the 007 special features. It was auctioned in London in 2010 for £2.6 million. Eon Productions sold the two show cars in 1969: one went to Canada where it was displayed at a restaurant until 1982; the other went to the USA where it remains. It is believed that the three cars continue in private ownership.

Other Bond films featuring the DB5 include *Goldeneye* (1995), *Tomorrow Never Dies* (1997) and *Skyfall* (2012), while in *Casino Royale* (2006) James Bond wins a DB5 in a poker game.

After the appearance of the DB5 in *Thunderball* the next Aston Martin to appear was the (then current) DBS, in the 1969 film *On Her Majesty's Secret Service*, which starred George Lazenby. In comparison with the DB5 the car had few items of special equipment and did not play a major part in the film.

Having missed the next nine productions an Aston Martin was then used in *The Living Daylights* (1987) with Timothy Dalton, this time a V8 Vantage. The car started as a Volante and was then changed into a saloon; it had skis,

The V8 Vantage from the 1987 film *The Living Daylights*.

missiles, rocket propulsion and the ability to self-destruct. The V8 Vantage is still owned by Eon.

The V12 Vanquish featured prominently in the 2002 film *Die Another Day* (with Bond played by Pierce Brosnan). The car has numerous special features including rockets, machine guns, a passenger ejector seat, the ability to become invisible and special spiked tyres for driving on ice. Seven cars were used in the film. Three were standard and were used for close-up photography, of which two have since been sold. Four were fitted with the gadgets noted above, Ford V8 engines and four-wheel drive; of these two were destroyed during filming, and it is thought that AML owns the others.

Casino Royale (2006) had a small part for the DB5 as already noted, but the main Aston Martin interest was the then new DBS with the V12 engine. There were few gadgets apart from storage for a pistol and a medical kit which

The V12 Vanquish from *Die Another Day* leaps across the ice, chased by Zao's Jaguar XKR.

included a defibrillator. A total of six cars were used, one of which met a spectacular end when it rolled seven times, this being entered in the *Guinness Book of Records*. The film's stunt crew found that the conventional method of using a ramp would not make the DBS roll, and so a gas-powered ram was used to produce the effect.

Daniel Craig and the DB5 in the 2012 film *Skyfall*.

Daniel Craig used a DBS again in the 2008 film *Quantum of Solace* when the car was severely damaged in a chase through Siena. Ten cars were used in the making of this film; one was destroyed and several others badly damaged.

In the film *Skyfall*, also starring Daniel Craig, the DB5 plays a significant role, culminating in its apparent destruction towards the end of the film. At least two cars were used, of which one (chassis number DB5/2007/R) is retained by AM Works.

FURTHER READING

Bowler, Michael. *Aston Martin V-8*. Cadogan, Guildford 1985.

Chudecki, Paul. *Aston Martin and Lagonda. Vol. 2: V8 models from 1970.* Motor Racing Publications, 1990.

Coram, Dudley. *Aston Martin: The Story of a Sports Car.* Motor Racing Publications, 1957.

Dowsey, David. *Aston Martin: Power, Beauty and Soul.* Peleus Press, 2010 (2nd edition).

Edwards, Robert. *Original Aston Martin DB4/5/6.* Bay View Books, 1992.

Hunter, Inman, *Aston Martin 1914 to 1940: A pictorial review.* Transport Bookman, 1976.

Hunter, Inman, with Archer, Alan. *Aston Martin 1913–1947.* Osprey, 1992.

Lillywhite, David, ed. *Aston Martin: The Complete Story.* Octane Media Ltd, 2009.

Murray, Neil. *On Aston Martin.* Palawan Press, 2005.

Nixon, Chris and Wyer, John. *Racing with the David Brown Aston Martins (Volumes 1 and 2).* Transport Bookman, 1980.

Noakes, Andrew. *Aston Martin DB7: The Complete Story.* The Crowood Press Ltd, 2006.

Presland, William. *Aston Martin V8.* The Crowood Press Ltd, 2009.

Pritchard, Anthony. *Aston Martin: A Racing History.* J. H. Haynes & Co. Ltd, 2006.

Tongue, Andy, ed. *AM The Aston Martin Yearbook 1913–2003: The Centenary Celebration.* Illustrated London News Ltd. for AML, 2013.

Whyte, Andrew. *The Aston Martin and Lagonda (Volume 1: Six-cylinder DB models).* Motor Racing Publications, 1984.

Worrall, Dave. *The Most Famous Car in the World.* Solo Publishing, 1993.

The Aston Martin Register – A listing of all Aston Martins manufactured, published by the Aston Martin Heritage Trust. The Registrar (Tim Cottingham) and his team are currently revising and updating the Register, which will allow it to be kept up to date and available online.

WEBSITES

There are numerous websites which refer to Aston Martin. The following will provide you with a good start and no doubt lead you towards many other useful links:

www.amht.org.uk The Aston Martin Heritage Trust

www.amoc.org The Aston Martin Owners Club

www.astonmartin.com The Aston Martin Lagonda company website

www.astonmartins.com An informative site run by Tim Cottingham

www.grandprixmodels.com   The well-respected retailer of car models and kits

www.smtsmodels.co.uk SMTS manufactures excellent quality metal models and kits.

PLACES TO VISIT

Aston Hill, near Tring in Hertfordshire. (The hill climb where Lionel Martin achieved good results in the early years; he used the name with his own for the company. A commemorative cairn was erected by the AMOC in 1997.)

Aston Martin Heritage Trust, The Barn, Drayton St Leonard, Wallingford, Oxfordshire OX10 7BG.
   Telephone: 01865 400414. Website: www.amht.org.uk (The AMHT is the official archive of Aston Martin. It owns the oldest existing B&M car (A3), a 1934 Ulster, the 1989 prototype AMR1 racing car and a 1972 AM Vantage; they are usually on display in the Barn. There is also a large collection of racing trophies, several engines, models and many interesting items of memorabilia. In addition the archive has a huge collection of images and documents covering the entire history of Aston Martin.)

Aston Martin Owners Club, The Barn, Drayton St Leonard, Wallingford, Oxfordshire OX10 7BG.
   Telephone: 01865 400400. Website: www.amoc.org
   (AMOC and AMHT race meetings, sprints, concours and other events as advertised on the websites and in the motoring press.)

Brooklands Museum, Brooklands Road, Weybridge, Surrey KT13 0QN.
   Telephone: 01932 857381. Website: www.brooklandsmuseum.com
   (Contains some of the original banked track from the world's first purpose-built racing circuit; three interesting B&M Aston Martins are also usually

on display – Razor Blade, the Halford Special and a three-seater, open-bodied, side-valve-engined road car.)

Coventry Transport Museum, Millennium Place, Hales Street, Coventry, Warwickshire CV1 1JD.

Telephone: 024 7623 4270. Website: www.transport-museum.com (Includes a prototype DB7)

Heritage Motor Centre, Banbury Road, Gaydon, Warwickshire CV35 0BJ.

Telephone: 01926 641188. Website: heritage-motor-centre.co.uk (An excellent collection of British-built cars; it usually includes several interesting Aston Martins.)

National Motor Museum, Beaulieu, Brockenhurst, Hampshire SO42 7ZN.

Telephone: 01590 612345. Website: www.beaulieu.co.uk. (Includes one of the 1922 Aston Martin Grand Prix cars.)

ABBREVIATIONS AND GLOSSARY

AMHT Aston Martin Heritage Trust

AML Aston Martin Lagonda

AMOC Aston Martin Owners Club

bhp brake horse power, a unit used to measure the power produced by an engine

B&M Bamford and Martin, the first company to make Aston-Martin cars

gullwing doors doors hinged at the top which open upwards and look rather like a bird's wings from the front of the car

LMP1 Le Mans Prototype, the top class of racing car in the Le Mans series of races

monocoque the hidden unitary structure to which the bodywork, interior and mechanical parts of a car are fitted

ohc overhead camshaft; the location of the camshaft(s) in an engine

shooting brake a coachbuilding term for an estate car

Team cars competition cars raced by Aston Martin's racing department

transaxle a combined gearbox (transmission) and differential (axle) fitted at the back on rear-wheel drive cars; widely used in mid-engined racing cars

TT Tourist Trophy, a motor race held in Ulster in the 1930s and later at Goodwood and then Silverstone

Vantage the name introduced in the David Brown era to denote cars with more powerful engines than standard, this was (usually) an extra cost option. In 1972 the name was used for a separate model; this occurred again in 2005 with the V8 Vantage and in 2009 with the V12 Vantage.

VH Vertical and Horizontal, a flexible design philosophy developed by AML which allowed different sizes of cars to share major components

Volante the name used by AML for its convertible cars from 1965

Works Service Renamed Aston Martin Works in 2012, this is based at Newport Pagnell and provides comprehensive after-sales service to customers. This ranges from routine maintenance, through full restoration, to bespoke engineering projects. A new car sales department was added in 2012.

INDEX